The Blessings of the Lord

Dr. Bala Success Abraham

Copyright © 2021 by **Dr. Bala Success Abraham**

All rights reserved. No part of this publication may be reproduced, distributed or transmitted in any form or by any means, including photocopying, recording, or other electronic or mechanical methods, without the prior written permission of the publisher, except in the case of brief quotations embodied in critical reviews and certain other noncommercial uses permitted by copyright law. For permission requests, write to the publisher, addressed "Attention: Permissions Coordinator," at the address below.

Dr. Bala Success Abraham/Rejoice Essential Publishing

PO BOX 512

Effingham, SC 29541

www.republishing.org

Unless otherwise indicated, scripture is taken from the King James Version.'

"Scripture quotations taken from the Amplified® Bible (AMP), Copyright © 2015 by The Lockman Foundation. Used by permission. www.lockman.org"

Scripture taken from the New King James Version®. Copyright © 1982 by Thomas Nelson. Used by permission. All rights reserved.

The Holy Bible, English Standard Version® (ESV®) Copyright © 2001 by Crossway, a publishing ministry of Good News Publishers. All rights reserved. ESV Text Edition: 2016

The Blessings of the Lord/Dr. Bala Success Abraham

ISBN-13: 978-1-956775-00-6

TABLE OF CONTENTS

ACKNOWLEDGMENT..vii

INTRODUCTION......................................1

CHAPTER 1: The Blessing, Not Your Labour............................7

CHAPTER 2: God Can Be Trusted...................16

CHAPTER 3: Abraham's Blessing....................24

CHAPTER 4: Wonders of The Blessing...........42

CHAPTER 5: How to Unlock The Blessing...50

CHAPTER 6: It Works...76

CHAPTER 7: Apostolic and Prophetic Declarations................................85

ABOUT THE AUTHOR...93

ACKNOWLEDGMENT

I ACKNOWLEDGE THE LORD OF the blessing, whose name is Jehovah El Shaddai. When we walk in covenant with El Shaddai, HE gives us the right to invoke His Name, the name of the one for whom nothing is impossible. I also want to thank my kingdom son, Dr. Emmanuel Jack, and his beautiful wife, Mercy. Immediately the inspiration came to me, and I called Dr. Jack, whose gift for writing helped me write this book.

I want to acknowledge my kingdom daughter Apostle Monica Sweeney, my ministerial assistant and coordinator of the Dallas Apostolic Triumphant church, and Pastor Blessing Ogidi. Also, I appreciate my kingdom daughter, the prophetess Hellena Vann, my Executive assistant for the Atlanta Branch. Thank you, Pastor Maria, for your commitment to the North Carolina Branch.

I also appreciate my kingdom son, pastor Kenneth of the South African Branch. Finally, I celebrate my leadership team in Lagos, Nigeria, our branch churches, and the Apostolic Team International (ATI) directors. The Blessing of the Lord will take you all to the top in Jesus' name. Amen.

INTRODUCTION

THE BLESSING OF THE LORD

"The blessing of the LORD, it maketh rich, and he addeth no sorrow with it." — Proverbs. 10:22

Many Christians do not understand the covenant of THE BLESSING of the LORD. Some believe that THE BLESSING of the LORD is the same thing as the blessings of God, but the two are not the same thing. The difference between them is not the suffix "s" but the covenant power behind - THE BLESSING.

THE BLESSING of the LORD goes beyond material things such as cars, houses, money, etc. These things are good in terms of making life

The Blessings of the Lord

comfortable and liveable. But they are not THE BLESSING of the LORD. Instead, THE BLESSING of the LORD is God's empowerment of a person to excel in all areas of life regardless of challenges, locality, and economic state of where the person resides.

On the other hand, the blessings of God are the natural things we receive from God, such as the free air we breathe, sunlight, rain, cars, houses, and natural things. The blessings of God are for all His creatures, including birds and shrubs.

As Jesus taught us, *"Jesus said, Therefore I say unto you, Take no thought for your life, what ye shall eat, or what ye shall drink; nor yet for your body, what ye shall put on, Is not the life more than meat, and the body than raiment? Behold the fowls of the air: for they sow not, neither do they reap, nor gather into barns; yet your heavenly Father feedeth them. Are ye not much better than they? Which of you by taking thought can add one cubit unto his stature? And why take ye thought for raiment? Consider the lilies of the field, how they grow; they toil not, neither do they spin: And yet I say unto you, That even Solomon in all his glory was not ar-*

rayed like one of these. Wherefore, if God so clothe the grass of the field, which today is, and tomorrow is cast into the oven, shall he not much more clothe you, O ye of little faith (Matthew 6:25-30)?"

Many unbelievers are rich in material possessions by dint of hard work. In terms of categorization, these are considered natural blessings. The Bible teaches us, *"THE BLESSING of the LORD goes beyond the natural things. It is a divinely-orchestrated power that enables people who are born of God to flourish physically, spiritually, materially, mentally and emotionally. The Bible says, But thou shalt remember the LORD thy God: for it is he that giveth thee power to get wealth, that he may establish his covenant which he sware unto thy fathers, as it is this day (Deuteronomy 8:18)."*

Right from creation, God gave man power to dominate his environment in its entirety. Believers who carry out this mandate to its logical conclusion exercise their divinely endowed power over their earthly enemies. Unbelievers have no portion in this mandate. Hence, they cannot pursue its realization nor experience such a supernatural dimension of life. This spiritual dimension is one of the reasons believers must stop envying the children of this world because their source of blessing is questionable. Besides, their spirituality is at its lowest. On the other hand, believers in Christ operate from a higher spiritual altitude than unbelievers because they sit together in heavenly places in Christ Jesus. Corroborating this truth, the Apostle Paul said, *"Even when we were dead in sins, hath quickened us together with Christ, And hath raised us up together, and made us sit together in heavenly places in Christ Jesus (Ephesians 2:5-6)."*

The wealth that comes from The BLESSING of the LORD has its roots in the womb of the Spirit. Therefore, it can't be stopped by natural forces or controlled by powers of darkness. Unbelievers cannot access this dimension of prosperity because they are not born of the Spirit. And natural minds cannot understand the things of the spirit. Accentuating this standpoint, the Apostle Paul said, *"But the natural man receiveth not the things of the Spirit of God: for they are foolishness unto him: neither can he know them, because they are spiritually discerned (1 Corinthians 2: 14)."*

INTRODUCTION

As stated earlier in the preceding paragraph, the Bible strictly warned that we should desist from being envious of unbelievers because of their wealth (Proverbs 24:1). This is because the wealth of the unbeliever is natural, transitional, and ephemeral. On the contrary, believers' wealth is a comprehensive insurance policy covering multi-dimensional needs, including having peace with God and favor, abundance, wisdom, joy, grace, freedom, and protection.

Those who truly understand the potency of THE BLESSING of the LORD have no reason to envy any unbeliever. The Bible teaches us, *"For I was envious at the foolish, when I saw the prosperity of the wicked. For there are no bands in their death: but their strength is firm. They are not in trouble as other men; neither are they plagued like other men. Therefore pride compasseth them about as a chain; violence covereth them as a garment. Their eyes stand out with fatness: they have more than heart could wish. They are corrupt, and speak wickedly concerning oppression: they speak loftily. They set their mouth against the heavens, and their tongue walketh through the earth. Therefore*

The Blessings of the Lord

his people return hither: and waters of a full cup are wrung out to them. And they say, How doth God know? and is there knowledge in the most High? Behold, these are the ungodly, who prosper in the world; they increase in riches. Verily I have cleansed my heart in vain, and washed my hands in innocency. For all the day long have I been plagued, and chastened every morning. If I say, I will speak thus; behold, I should offend against the generation of thy children. When I thought to know this, it was too painful for me; Until I went into the sanctuary of God; then understood I their end. Surely thou didst set them in slippery places: thou castedst them down into destruction. How are they brought into desolation, as in a moment! they are utterly consumed with terrors (Psalm 73:3-19)."

In Chapter 1, we shall see the superiority of THE BLESSING of the LORD over man's labor.

CHAPTER 1

THE BLESSING, NOT YOUR LABOUR

"Except the LORD build the house, they labour in vain that build it: except the LORD keep the city, the watchman waketh but in vain. It is vain for you to rise up early, to sit up late, to eat the bread of sorrows: for so he giveth his beloved sleep." — *Psalms 127:1-2*

God in His wisdom did not create man to succeed independent of Himself. From the story of creation, it is clear that God is the source of man's existence. That means man relies on God

The Blessings of the Lord

for His needs. From creation, God's plan will empower and sustain man to reign and have dominion over His creation. What He did was to put THE BLESSING upon Adam and Eve to activate God's nature in them. Most people, including some preachers, are ignorant that the last thing God did during creation was not the creation of man but the blessing or empowerment of man.

"So God created man in his own image, in the image of God created he him; male and female created he them. And God blessed them, and God said unto them, Be fruitful, and multiply, and replenish the earth, and subdue it: and have dominion over the fish of the sea, and over the fowl of the air, and over every living thing that moveth upon the earth (Genesis 1:27-28)."

When you understand this perspective of the creation of man, it will reset your mind and cause you to appreciate the wisdom of God and His love for humanity. The dominion and superiority of man over other creatures came when God pronounced THE BLESSING upon them. After this encounter, Adam was able to name all the animals without any form of assistance. The Bible reminds us of this momentous encounter. *"And out of the ground the LORD God formed every beast of the field, and every fowl of the air; and brought them unto Adam to see what he would call them: and whatsoever Adam called every living creature, that was the name thereof. And Adam gave names to all cattle, and to the fowl of the air, and to every beast of the field; but for Adam there was not found an help meet for him. And out of the ground the LORD God formed every beast of the field, and every fowl of the air; and brought them unto Adam to see what he would call them: and whatsoever Adam called every living creature, that was the name thereof. And Adam gave names to all cattle, and to the fowl of the air, and to every beast of the field; but for Adam there was not found an help meet for him (Genesis 2:19-20)."*

At this stage, Adam was operating like God. Consequently, every creature submitted to him. A school of thought postulates that all animals took their character and characteristics from Adam's names. For example, lions, sheep, goats, monkeys were the same. They had no direction and definite function until Adam gave them names. It was these names that activated their characters and behaviors. Whether it is true or not, one important and undeniable fact is that Adam exercised his God-given authority and discretion over creation. All of this was made possible as a result of THE BLESSING God pronounced on him.

VICTORY OVER SIN

When Adam and Eve sinned against God in the Garden of Eden by disobeying His instruction, there was a shift! Adam plummeted from his lofty position of authority and lost his position in the Garden of Eden. Adam and Eve lived in dread of the creatures that once submitted to their authority from that moment. From this point, poverty, sickness, and physical death into the world.

GOOD NEWS

The fall of man brought devastating effects on the world, especially on humanity. Even though Adam woes upon himself and the entire world, God in His preserved THE BLESSING that He put upon Adam. In one of his teachings, Kenneth Copeland described THE BLESSING OF THE LORD as "the Gospel." He added that "sin changed everything except God." Despite the sinfulness, God chose to preserve His relationship with us. The Bible reflects that decision, *"For I am the LORD, I change not; therefore ye sons of Jacob are not consumed (Malachi 3:6)."* And again, *"Every good gift and every perfect gift is from above, and cometh down from the Father of lights, with whom is no variableness, neither shadow of turning (James 1:17)."*

Since God does not change, His love and original plan for humanity also have not changed. Therefore, God took the responsibility of ensuring that THE BLESSING (the Gospel), which is empowerment, remains potent. God has seen fit this power is given to us freely. Paul writes, *"For I am not ashamed of the Gospel of Christ: for it is the power of God unto salvation to everyone that believeth; to the Jew first, and also to the Greek (Romans 1:16)."*

Through wisdom, power, and love, God passed THE BLESSING from one generation to another until our Jesus Christ was born. And through Him, THE BLESSING on humanity was fully restored.

THE BLESSING IS THE ACTIVATOR

It is THE BLESSING of the LORD that makes you rich, not your labor. This fact is critical to our breakthrough in life. Hard work is excellent and commendable, but that alone cannot secure your prosperity as God intended. It is our faith in God that connects us to God. The Bible teaches us, *"And thou say in thine heart, My power and the might of mine hand hath gotten me this wealth. But thou shalt remember the LORD thy God: for it is he that giveth thee power to get wealth, that he may establish his covenant which he sware unto thy fathers, as it is this day (Deuteronomy 8:11-18)."*

I believe in hard work. I have never been slothful in business. As a church worker, I worked and served my pastor and others. I evangelized my community and won souls for the Lord to the extent that people thought I worked for the church. But it was just my passion and love for the Lord that were my driving forces.

In the military, I worked so hard that all my superiors and juniors loved me with passion. They did not only admire my diligence, but they also had confidence in my ability and truthfulness. In my days back in school, I was never lazy. Despite many challenges that confronted me in school then, I stayed focused on my studies. As a minister of the Gospel, I have many assignments: I co-ordinate our headquarters church in Atlanta and branches in America, Nigeria, South Africa, etc. I also provide leadership oversight to many churches on the African continent.

So, I understand what hard work entails. However, what supplies the anointing, energy, grace, finances, and victory for my team and me is THE BLESSING of The LORD, not my labor. The Apostle Paul believed the same when he said: *"But by the grace of God I am what I am: and his grace which was bestowed upon me was not in vain; but I laboured more abundantly than they all: yet not I, but the grace of God which was with me (1 Corinthians 15:10)."*

The Blessings of the Lord

It is good to be diligent, but diligence alone cannot make you. It cannot give you velocity and divine acceleration. It cannot provide you anointing and audacity. It cannot cast out demons. It cannot heal the sick nor raise the dead. So many diligent, skillful and intelligent people but unable to discover their destinies, let alone fulfill them. God is your source, not your business. If you depend on your business, skills, etc., you will go down with it when your business is overwhelmed with challenges. Regardless of what happens in your environment, you will bounce forward in every situation if you make God your source. The Bible teaches us, *"And we know that all things work together for good to them that love God, to them who are the called according to his purpose (Romans 8:28)."* And again, *"For whatsoever is born of God overcometh the world: and this is the victory that overcometh the world, even our faith. (1 John 5:4)."*

The BLESSING of the LORD, not our labor, makes us rich and adds no sorrow. Therefore, THE BLESSING is the place to be.

In the next chapter, we shall see how God remained faithful to His promise by ensuring that THE BLESSING was unaffected by the challenges that confronted the carriers of THE BLESSING from generation to generation until Christ was born.

CHAPTER 2

GOD CAN BE TRUSTED

"God is not a man, that he should lie; neither the son of man, that he should repent: hath he said, and shall he not do it? or hath he spoken, and shall he not make it good" — Numbers 23:19

Our God is the Omnipotent, Omnipresent, and Wise God. He is the Alpha and the Omega. Nothing takes Him unaware. For example, when He put THE BLESSING on Adam and Eve, He also knew they would mess things up. To that extent, He put a safety measure in place to protect THE BLESSING (Gospel) from being destroyed. As indicated in the previous chapter, God successfully passed it from Adam through many generations until it got to Christ rather than destroy THE BLESSING.

THE BLESSING that God pronounced on Adam made him a co-creator with God. Adam was empowered to continue to create things that were not in existence at his creation. The pronouncement of THE BLESSING made the fulfillment of the assignment given to him by God in Genesis 1:28 both a spiritual and material reality. After putting THE BLESSING on Adam and Eve, God rested. Why would He do that? The simple reason is that God had confidence in Adam. He knew that THE BLESSING would teach Adam what to do. So the Bible says, *"And God blessed them, and God said unto them, Be fruitful, and multiply, and replenish the earth, and subdue it: and have dominion over the fish of the sea, and over the fowl of the air, and over every living thing that moveth upon the earth..... Thus the heavens and the earth were finished, and all the host of them. And on the seventh day God ended his work which he had made; and he rested on the seventh day from all his work which he had made. And God blessed the seventh day, and sanctified it: because that in it he had rested from all his*

The Blessings of the Lord

work which God created and made (Genesis 1:28; 2:1-3)."

A great teacher on THE BLESSING said, "Contrary to popular belief, God wasn't commanding Adam and Eve just to have babies. The phrase "be fruitful, and multiply" means to increase and have abundance in every way. Replenish means "to perpetually renew, supply." When God spoke these words, He endowed humanity with the divine power to increase and excel in everything good. He empowered them to fill the earth with that goodness. I assumed for years that God had so thoroughly completed the planet that all Adam and Eve had to do was pluck ripe fruit from the trees and enjoy themselves. I figured that because the Garden of Eden was a perfect place, there must not have been much for them to do. That would have been true if the Garden had covered the whole earth."

When Adam sinned, THE BLESSING could not produce abundantly for him because the devil took hold of the earth contrary to God's original plan and purpose for man. As a result, the earth began to work against him because of

God's curse upon the ground. The Bible reminds us of this tragic scene in Genesis 3:14-15, 17-19, *"And the LORD God said unto the serpent, Because thou hast done this, thou art cursed above all cattle, and above every beast of the field; upon thy belly shalt thou go, and dust shalt thou eat all the days of thy life. And I will put enmity between thee and the woman, and between thy seed and her seed; it shall bruise thy head, and thou shalt bruise his heel....And unto Adam he said, Because thou hast hearkened unto the voice of thy wife, and hast eaten of the tree, of which I commanded thee, saying, Thou shalt not eat of it: cursed is the ground for thy sake; in sorrow shalt thou eat of it all the days of thy life; Thorns also and thistles shall it bring forth to thee; and thou shalt eat the herb of the field; In the sweat of thy face shalt thou eat bread, till thou return unto the ground; for out of it wast thou taken: for dust thou art, and unto dust shalt thou return."*

God did not curse man directly. Instead, He dealt with the circumstances Adam and Eve created. Nevertheless, the curse came as a shock to them because of what their actions caused. Death, sickness, and poverty were strange and foreign to them. No doubt, they must have been wondering how they would ever get out of that gory situation. Things continued like this for a while.

As time went by, Adam and Eve bore children. With the increase of the population of human beings on earth, things became worse as sin and suffering multiplied. The situation was so sad and pathetic that God said, *"My spirit shall not always strive with man, for that he also is flesh: yet his days shall be an hundred and twenty years. There were giants in the earth in those days; and also after that, when the sons of God came in unto the daughters of men, and they bare children to them, the same became mighty men which were of old, men of renown. And GOD saw that the wickedness of man was great in the earth, and that every imagination of the thoughts of his heart was only evil continually. And it repented the LORD that he had made man on the earth, and it grieved him at his heart. And the LORD said, I will destroy man whom I have created from the face of the earth; both man, and beast, and the creeping thing, and the fowls of the air; for it repenteth me that I have made them (Genesis 6:3-7)."*

The statement above does not imply that God regretted creating man. If this were true, He would have wiped them off from the earth with a wave of His hand. Also, if this theology is true, then the integrity of God is suspect because the word of God introduced Him as the God of love and compassion. Therefore, God did not regret man's existence. Instead, God regretted that man lived under a curse instead of THE BLESSING He originally planned for him.

NOAH

In this perverse world, Noah found grace in the eyes of the Lord, for God found him righteous. So God commissioned Noah to build an ark to save his family from the torrential rain about to fall upon the earth. And the Bible tells us that *"Noah did as God instructed him. His household, two of each animals species (male and female) and himself were in the ark while it rained thunderously for 40 days until the whole earth was covered by water and all living things died (Genesis 8:13-24)."*

The Blessings of the Lord

GOD BLESSED NOAH

After the waters receded, Noah, his household, and the animals disembarked from the ark; God again pronounced THE BLESSING upon them. The Bible teaches us, *"And God blessed Noah and his sons, and said unto them, Be fruitful, and multiply, and replenish the earth. And the fear of you and the dread of you shall be upon every beast of the earth, and upon every fowl of the air, upon all that moveth upon the earth, and upon all the fishes of the sea; into your hand are they delivered. Every moving thing that liveth shall be meat for you; even as the green herb have I given you all things....And you, be ye fruitful, and multiply; bring forth abundantly in the earth, and multiply therein. And God spake unto Noah, and to his sons with him, saying, And I, behold, I establish my covenant with you, and with your seed after you; And with every living creature that is with you, of the fowl, of the cattle, and of every beast of the earth with you; from all that go out of the ark, to every beast of the earth. And I will establish my covenant with you; neither shall all flesh be cut off any more by the waters of a flood; neither shall there any more be a flood to destroy the earth (Genesis 9:1-3, 7-11)."*

God put upon Adam and Eve this same BLESSING. Noah needed THE BLESSING if the plan of God for humanity was going to work. Now with THE BLESSING placed upon Noah, the earth was on a path to restoration. When Noah and his family had settled down, like Adam and Eve, Noah and his sons messed things up. As a result, his sons wandered from the path of righteousness. Ham and Japheth became carnal-minded and invented a new way of doing business

THE BLESSING God pronounced on Adam made him a co-creator with God, independent of God as his source. But it was Noah's first son, Shem, who continued on the path of righteousness. Thus, THE BLESSING of the LORD continued to work through the bloodline or descendants of Shem. It's important to note that Abram, who later became Abraham, the father of faith, came from the lineage of Shem. In the next chapter, we shall discuss how God passed THE BLESSING to Abraham and how that has impacted the world.

CHAPTER 3

ABRAHAM'S BLESSING

"And if ye be Christ's, then are ye Abraham's seed, and heirs according to the promise." — Galatians 3:29

The first time God spoke to Abram, he and his family lived at Ur. The people of Ur at that time were idol worshippers. God instructed him to move out of the heathen city of Ur to a place He would show him. The separation was necessary because God did not want him and THE BLESSING corrupted. He also wanted to reset his mind to think differently from the people of Ur. God wanted him to begin to think in line with his new status. God's demand for His chosen vessels has also been to separate from the world and remain holy unto Him.

The command for God's people to be holy by remaining separate from the world is specific. In Ezra 10:10-11, the Bible teaches us, *"And Ezra the priest stood up, and said unto them, "Ye have transgressed, and have taken strange wives, to increase the trespass of Israel. Now therefore make confession unto the LORD God of your fathers, and do his pleasure: and separate yourselves from the people of the land, and from the strange wives."*

And Paul continues this teaching of holiness through separation through the explicit comparison between righteousness and unrighteousness. Paul writes in 2 Corinthians 6:14-17, *"Be ye not unequally yoked together with unbelievers: for what fellowship hath righteousness with unrighteousness? and what communion hath light with darkness? And what concord hath Christ with Belial? or what part hath he that believeth with an infidel? And what agreement hath the temple of God with idols? for ye are the temple of the living God; as God hath said, I will dwell in them, and walk in them; and I will be their God, and they shall be*

The Blessings of the Lord

my people. Wherefore come out from among them, and be ye separate, saith the Lord, and touch not the unclean thing; and I will receive you."

The next thing God did after asking Abraham to move away from his country, his kindred and from his father's house was to bless him. Now the LORD had said unto Abram, *"Get thee out of thy country, and from thy kindred, and from thy father's house, unto a land that I will shew thee: And I will make of thee a great nation, and I will bless thee, and make thy name great; and thou shalt be a blessing; And I will bless them that bless thee, and curse him that curseth thee: and in thee shall all families of the earth be blessed. So Abram departed, as the LORD had spoken unto him; and Lo went with him: and Abram was seventy and five years old when he departed out of Haran (Genesis 12:1-4)."*

THE BLESSING God put on Abram, who later became Abraham was the same BLESSING He put on Adam and Noah. God chose Abraham probably because He saw his faith and knew that he would teach his children the ways of God. Moreover, he knew that with Abraham,

THE BLESSING would pass on to his natural and spiritual descendants. So God told him, "*In thee shall all families of the earth be blessed....*" (Genesis 12:3b) And as Abraham believed and obeyed, THE BLESSING began working immediately in the life of Abraham and his household. His nephew, Lot, also began to prosper, *"And Lot also, which went with Abram, had flocks, and herds, and tents. And the land was not able to bear them, that they might dwell together: for their substance was great, so that they could not dwell together (Genesis 13:5-6)."*

Although THE BLESSING took place almost immediately, the full manifestation of it came after Abraham had separated from Lot, whom he carried along when he left Ur. Genesis 13:14-18 tells us, *"And the LORD said unto Abram, after that Lot was separated from him, Lift up now thine eyes, and look from the place where thou art northward, and southward, and eastward, and westward: And the LORD said unto Abram, after that Lot was separated from him, Lift up now thine eyes, and look from the place where thou art northward, and southward, and eastward, and westward: And I will make thy seed as the dust of the earth: so that if a man can number the dust of the earth, then shall thy seed also be numbered. Arise, walk through the land in the length of it and in the breadth of it; for I will give it unto thee. Then Abram removed his tent, and came and dwelt in the plain of Mamre, which is in Hebron, and built there an altar unto the LORD."*

THE BLESSING will not produce maximally in your life until you learn to obey the word of God. *"He openeth also their ear to discipline, and commandeth that they return from iniquity. If they obey and serve him, they shall spend their days in prosperity, and their years in pleasures. But if they obey not, they shall perish by the sword, and they shall die without knowledge (Job 36:10-12)."* Again God's word instructs us, saying, *"If ye be willing and obedient, ye shall eat the good of the land: But if ye refuse and rebel, ye shall be devoured with the sword: for the mouth of the LORD hath spoken it (Isaiah 1:19-20)."*

DIVINE REVELATION

By all standards, Abraham was blessed. He was victorious in every battle. His business prospered, and his servants were in top form. However, Abraham did not fully understand the impact of THE BLESSING God placed upon him until he encountered Melchizedek, king of Salem, after his victory over Chedorlaomer. Genesis 14:18-20 records that meeting, *"And Melchizedek king of Salem brought forth bread and wine: and he was the priest of the most high God. And he blessed him, and said, Blessed be Abram of the most high God, possessor of heaven and earth: And blessed be the most high God, which hath delivered thine enemies into thy hand. And he gave him tithes of all."*

During this encounter, Abraham knew that THE BLESSING God put on him was natural blessings and divine empowerment. He had been made "possessor of heaven and earth" through that pronouncement by God. This new understanding ignited his faith and audacity for exploits and made his faith in God stronger than ever.

THE RIGHTEOUS IS AS BOLD AS LION

The Blessings of the Lord

When Abraham received THE BLESSING, which is the Gospel, he also received anointing for boldness and audacity along with it. This boldness was the reason Abraham was able to lift his hands to the Lord, set his face like a flint, and declared to the king of Sodom that he would not take anything from him lest he should say, "I have made Abram rich." *And the king of Sodom said unto Abram, Give me the persons, and take the goods to thyself. And Abram said to the king of Sodom, I have lifted up mine hand unto the LORD, the most high God, the possessor of heaven and earth, That I will not take from a thread even to a shoe latchet, and that I will not take any thing that is thine, lest thou shouldest say, I have made Abram rich: Save only that which the young men have eaten, and the portion of the men which went with me, Aner, Eshcol, and Mamre; let them take their portion (Genesis 14:21-24)."*

Genuine salvation usually produces boldness in the life of the believer. A believer's boldness is the supernatural result of the indwelling Holy Spirit and the Word of God.

"The wicked flee when no man pursueth: but the righteous are bold as a lion." — Proverbs 28:1

"Now when they saw the boldness of Peter and John, and perceived that they were unlearned and ignorant men, they marvelled; and they took knowledge of them, that they had been with Jesus" — Acts 4:13 KJV

"And when they had prayed, the place was shaken where they were assembled together; and they were all filled with the Holy Ghost, and they spake the word of THE BLESSING God put on Abram who God with boldness." — Acts 4:31 KJV

This is when the boldness of the faithful believer empowered with THE BLESSING changes the world.

TITHE AND THE BLESSING

Before we proceed, let's look at one important thing Abraham did when he encountered Melchizedek and revealed knowledge of THE BLESSING. He responded by giving him 10 percent or a tithe of all he had. Why did Abraham

The Blessings of the Lord

do that? The Spirit of God must have revealed this to him. Don't forget that God was trying to establish a new way of life on earth. Abraham was the connecting rod between divinity and humanity. The blessing God put on Abram was the same BLESSING God put on Adam and Noah. He was the one with the mantle of THE BLESSING. Therefore, it was natural for God to reveal this covenant principle to him.

"And the king of Sodom went out to meet him after his return from the slaughter of Chedorlaomer, and of the kings that were with him, at the valley of Shaveh, which is the king's dale. And Melchizedek king of Salem brought forth bread and wine: and he was the priest of the most high God. And he blessed him, and said, Blessed be Abram of the most high God, possessor of heaven and earth: And blessed be the most high God, which hath delivered thine enemies into thy hand. And he gave him tithes of all (Genesis 14:17-20)."

"For this Melchizedec, king of Salem, priest of the most high God, who met Abraham returning from the slaughter of the kings, and blessed him; To whom also Abraham gave a tenth part of all;

first being by interpretation King of righteousness, and after that also King of Salem, which is, King of peace; Without father, without mother, without descent, having neither beginning of days, nor end of life; but made like unto the Son of God; abideth a priest continually (Hebrews 7:1-4)."

Many people still believe that tithing is of the Old Testament and unnecessary in the era of grace, but that is not true. The tithe started in the Garden of Eden and continued with Abraham, which happened several years before the advent of the Mosaic law.

While teaching on tithing, Kenneth Copeland said, "Contrary to what some have taught, the concept of tithing didn't originate with the law of Moses. It originated in the Garden of Eden." That's why in Genesis 4, we find Abel bringing God the firstborn of his flock. Although Abel lived thousands of years before the law, somehow, he learned to tithe. Who taught him? There's only one possible answer. It must have been his father. Adam wanted his children to avoid the heartbreaking, life-wrecking sin he had committed, so he instructed them to give God the first and best portion of their increase.

Abel understood and applied what Adam told him. His brother Cain, however, didn't. What happened between them as a result reveals just how vital the principle of tithing truly is." The tithe is a very important part of the covenant of THE BLESSING of the LORD. You will never experience all of THE BLESSING of the LORD if you don't Tithe. THE BLESSING is God's prerogative and gift to us, while tithe is the expression of our love; THE BLESSING will not produce maximally in your life until you learn to obey the word of God. The tithe is your covenant responsibility for THE BLESSING to continue to flourish in your life. Principles rule the world, and once you break any of these principles, you would suffer the consequences.

You must be careful not to allow man's theology or ideology, personal needs, Abraham's, and challenges to stop you from fulfilling this covenant responsibility of giving your tithe. If you fail to do so, THE BLESSING of God upon your life will not produce maximally.

For more studies on tithing, read 30 Questions And Answers On Tithing by Dr. Emmanuel Jack.

HOW ABRAHAM RECEIVED THE BLESSING

Abraham received THE BLESSING by believing what God said. It was not because of what he did; it was because of the unmerited favor of God that he enjoyed. The point is this: THE BLESSING belonged to him, but he had to receive it by faith. He had to believe in the integrity of God's word. So, it was his faith that allowed God to establish the promise in his life.

God's demand for His chosen vessels has also been to separate from the world and remain holy unto Him. All the descendants of Abraham who trusted the covenant of THE BLESSING and kept God's commandment also walked in THE BLESSING. They were not just prosperous; they were exceedingly prosperous. You cannot walk in THE BLESSING if you do not believe God's Word concerning prosperity.

THE BLESSINGS OF THE LORD

"These are the words of the covenant, which the LORD commanded Moses to make with the children of Israel in the land of Moab, beside the covenant which he made with them in Horeb ... Keep therefore the words of this covenant, and do them, that ye may prosper in all that ye do (Deuteronomy 29:1, 9)."

GOD'S DESIRE

God desires to establish THE BLESSING on earth. He did this under the old covenant without any challenge. He blessed Abraham and his descendants as He had promised in Genesis 12:1-4,

"And when Abram was ninety years old and nine, the LORD appeared to Abram, and said unto him, I am the Almighty God; walk before me, and be thou perfect. And I will make my covenant between me and thee, and will multiply thee exceedingly. AndAbram fell on his face: and God talked with him, saying, As for me, behold, my covenant is with thee, and thou shalt be an Abraham's Blessing *father of many nations. Neither shall thy name any*

more be called Abram, but thy name shall be Abraham; for a father of many nations have I made thee. And I will make thee exceeding fruitful, and I will make nations of thee, and kings shall come out of thee. And I will establish my covenant between me and thee and thy seed after thee in their generations for an everlasting covenant, to be a God unto thee, and to thy seed after thee. And I will give unto thee, and to thy seed after thee, the land wherein thou art a stranger, all the land of Canaan, for an everlasting possession; and I will be their God. And God said unto Abraham, Thou shalt keep my covenant therefore, thou, and thy seed after thee in their generations (Genesis 17:1-9)."

ISAAC

The Bible tells us that Isaac became great and very prosperous.

God established His covenant of BLESSING with Abraham and his seed after him in their generations. *"But my covenant will I establish with Isaac, which Sarah shall bear unto thee at this set time in the next year (Genesis 17:21)."*

THE BLESSINGS OF THE LORD

"And the LORD appeared unto him the same night, and said, I am the God of Abraham thy father: fear not, for I am with thee, and will bless thee, and multiply thy seed for my servant Abraham's sake (Genesis 26:24)."

"And the man waxed great, and went forward, and grew until he became very great: For he had possession of flocks, and possession of herds, and great store of servants: and the Philistines envied him (Genesis 26:13-14)."

JACOB

God also established Abraham's BLESSING in Jacob's life. As a result, Jacob increased and became exceedingly rich.

"And the man increased exceedingly, and had much cattle, and maidservants, and menservants, and camels, and asses (Genesis 30:43)."

JOSEPH

Joseph prospered everywhere he went. The bars of a prison, nor the laws of Egypt, could not stop his prosperity. THE BLESSING of the LORD can work anywhere. It is not limited to a particular locality.

"And the LORD was with Joseph, and he was a prosperous man; and he was in the house of his master the Egyptian. And his master saw that the LORD was with him, and that the LORD made all that he did to prosper in his hand (Genesis 39:2-3)."

"As a carrier of THE BLESSING, Daniel also prospered in his days. So David waxed greater and greater: for the LORD of hosts was with him (1 Chronicles 11:9)."

As long as a believer keeps the covenant, THE BLESSING of the LORD cannot be stopped in the life of Abraham's heirs.

THE BLOOD OF JESUS

Through the supreme sacrifice of Jesus on the cross, the Gentiles have are part of God's family. Jesus' death on the cross made both the

THE BLESSINGS OF THE LORD

Jews and the Gentiles children of God and partakers of Abraham's BLESSING.

"Christ hath redeemed us from the curse of the law, being made a curse for us: for it is written, Cursed is everyone that hangeth on a tree: That the blessing of Abraham might come on the Gentiles through Jesus Christ; that we might receive the promise of the Spirit through faith (Genesis 3:13-14)."

The blood of Jesus qualifies us to become partakers of Abraham's BLESSING, which was the same BLESSING that God put upon Adam and Noah.

"For ye are all the children of God by faith in Christ Jesus. For as many of you as have been baptized into Christ have put on Christ. There is neither Jew nor Greek, there is neither bond nor free, there is neither male nor female: for ye are all one in Christ Jesus. And if ye be Christ's, then are ye Abraham's seed, and heirs according to the promise (Galatians 3:26-29)."

ABRAHAM'S BLESSING

Abraham's covenant is everlasting. As an heir to THE BLESSING of Abraham, God is willing to establish His covenant with us today as surely as He did with Abraham, Isaac, and Jacob. We have already received the redemption of our spirit. Therefore, we must grow in knowledge and obedience to the word of God to receive our inheritance to have all our needs (spirit, soul, and body) met by the power of the Spirit. The blood of Jesus qualifies us to become partakers of Abraham's BLESSING, which was the same BLESSING that God put upon Adam and Noah.

In the next chapter, we shall discuss the wonders of THE BLESSING of the LORD

CHAPTER 4

WONDERS OF THE BLESSING

"And it shall come to pass, if thou shalt hearken diligently unto the voice of the LORD thy God, to observe and to do all his commandments which I command thee this day, that the LORD thy God will set thee on high above all nations of the earth."
— Deuteronomy 28:1

Earlier in the book, I stated that THE BLESSING of the LORD is different from the blessings of God. I said that THE BLESSING of the LORD is not cars, houses, money, and other natural things. I know that many readers will wonder if those are not THE BLESSING, then what is THE BLESSING?

THE BLESSINGS OF THE LORD

THE BLESSING is divine empowerment placed upon a person by God to dominate regardless of the forces fighting against him. I know that I have said this before. However, I am repeating it because of the other truths I'm about to reveal now.

The honest and straightforward answer to the above question is that material things are part of THE BLESSING of the LORD. However, THE BLESSING of the LORD is not limited to natural things. God had a bigger picture in mind when He established the covenant of THE BLESSING on earth. He wanted humanity to excel both in the spiritual and the physical worlds. He wanted humanity to have dominion over the spiritual and physical worlds.

God never wanted man to run around begging for miracles. Rather, He wanted him to be a creator of miracles.

"Behold, I and the children whom the LORD hath given me are for signs and for wonders in

THE BLESSINGS OF THE LORD

Israel from the LORD of hosts, which dwelleth in mount Zion (Isaiah 8:18)."

God never wanted man to move from one place to the other, seeking blessings. Instead, God wanted man to be the blessing. That was why He put THE BLESSING on Adam, Noah, Abraham, and his descendants.

PROSPERITY IS THE WILL OF GOD

Prosperity is the will of God for us. But God wants us to be more than wealthy. He wants us to channel THE BLESSING so that God's power is manifest. So that when we boast, it is all because of God.

"Beloved, I wish above all things that thou mayest prosper and be in health, even as thy soul prospereth (3 John 2)."

"Every good gift and every perfect gift is from above, and cometh down from the Father of lights, with whom is no variableness, neither shadow of turning. (James 1:17)."

God is the author of every good thing, and He wants us to have them. But the prosperity that comes from God must come through the covenant He established with Abraham, not our labor or satanic manipulations. That is why He urged the people of Israel not to forget their source.

"But thou shalt remember the LORD thy God: for it is he that giveth thee power to get wealth, that he may establish his covenant which he sware unto thy fathers, as it is this day (Deuteronomy 8:18)."

The source of our prosperity is not our skill, labor, or business. Your ability cannot command the dimensions of blessing God intends for humanity.

"Except the LORD build the house, they labour in vain that build it: except the LORD keep the city, the watchman waketh but In vain. It is vain for you to rise up early, to sit up late, to eat the bread of sorrows: for so he giveth his beloved sleep (Psalms 127:1-2)."

THE BLESSINGS OF THE LORD

The source of our prosperity is the Spirit of God, which is why THE BLESSING IS unstoppable.

"Then he answered and spake unto me, saying, This is the word of the LORD unto Zerubbabel, saying, Not by might, nor by power, but by my Spirit, saith the LORD of hosts (Zechariah 4:6)."

As we walk in the Spirit, the covenant of THE BLESSING of the LORD will continue to prosper us.

"And it shall be, if thou do at all forget the LORD thy God, and walk after other the LORD thy God, to observe and to do all his commandments which I command thee this day, that the LORD thy God will set thee on high above all nations of the earth: And all these blessings shall come on thee, and overtake thee, if thou shalt hearken unto the voice of the LORD thy God (Deuteronomy 8:19-20)."

"Blessed shalt thou be in the city, and blessed shalt thou be in the field. Blessed shall be the fruit of thy body, and the fruit of thy ground, and the fruit of thy cattle, the increase of thy kine, and the

flocks of thy sheep. Blessed shall be thy basket and thy store. Blessed shalt thou be when thou comest in, and blessed shalt thou be when thou goest out. The LORD shall cause thine enemies that rise up against thee to be smitten before thy face: they shall come out against thee one way, and flee before thee seven ways. The LORD shall command the blessing upon thee in thy storehouses, and in all that thou settest thine hand unto; and he shall bless thee in the land which the LORD thy God giveth thee. The LORD shall establish thee an holy people unto himself, as he hath sworn unto thee, if thou shalt keep the commandments of the LORD thy God, and walk in his ways. And all people of the earth shall see that thou art called by the name of the LORD; and they shall be afraid of thee. And the LORD shall make thee plenteous in goods, in the fruit of thy body, and in the fruit of thy cattle, and in the fruit of thy ground, in the land which the LORD sware unto thy fathers to give thee. The LORD shall open unto thee his good treasure, the heaven to give the rain unto thy land in his season, and to bless all the work of thine hand: and thou shalt lend unto many nations, and thou shalt not borrow. And the LORD shall make thee the head, and not the tail; and thou shalt be above only, and

THE BLESSINGS OF THE LORD

thou shalt not be beneath; if that thou hearken unto the commandments of the LORD thy God, which I command thee this day, to observe and to do them: And thou shalt not go aside from any of the words which I command thee this day, to the right hand, or to the left, to go after other gods to serve them (Deuteronomy 28:1-14)."

These benefits are products of THE BLESSING. A careful study of this passage reveals that they are far beyond material gains. They are multi-dimensional, covering the spiritual, physical, social, financial, and emotional needs of man. Only God can do this. But for the blessing to continue, the Israelites only had to obey the commands of the Lord.

"And it shall be, if thou do at all forget the LORD thy God, and walk after other gods, and serve them, and worship them, I testify against you this day that ye shall surely perish. As the nations which the LORD destroyeth before your face, so shall ye perish; because ye would not be obedient unto the voice of the LORD your God (Deuteronomy 8:19-20)."

Everything you will ever need is in THE BLESSING of the LORD, which is the Gospel. Once you have received THE BLESSING of the LORD, it will bless your life. The blessings of God are in THE BLESSING of the LORD and not the other way round.

In chapter 5, we shall examine how to unlock THE BLESSING to produce in our lives. THE BLESSING of the LORD is not limited to natural things.

CHAPTER 5

HOW TO UNLOCK THE BLESSING

"And ye shall know the truth, and the truth shall make you free." — John 8:32

THE BLESSING of the LORD is upon us as believers in Christ. Jesus made this possible by offering Himself as a sacrifice in our place. The Apostle Paul said, *"Christ hath redeemed us from the curse of the law, being made a curse for us: for it is written, Cursed is everyone that hangeth on a tree: That the blessing of Abraham might come on the Gentiles through Jesus Christ; that we might receive the promise of the Spirit through faith (Galatians 3:13-14)."*

HOW TO UNLOCK THE BLESSING

Every believer in Christ has THE BLESSING securely placed upon him, but its manifestation depends on individual Christians. The degree to which each Christian will experience the manifestation of THE BLESSING varies. And this can be traced to several factors.

Prominent among these factors are ignorance, wrong belief, and disobedience. Before we discuss how we can unlock THE BLESSING, let's take a cursory look at such factors.

1. IGNORANCE

Being ignorant does not mean someone is stupid. Simply put, ignorance is a lack of knowledge. For example, someone can be a professor of medicine but ignorant of soap-making processes. This type of ignorance is excusable because no one has a monopoly on knowledge.

On the contrary, spiritual ignorance is expensive because it has deadly and dire consequences. Hence, God said, *"My people are destroyed for lack of knowledge: because thou hast rejected knowledge, I will also reject thee, that thou shalt be no priest to me: seeing thou hast forgotten the law of thy God, I will also forget thy children (Hosea 4:6 KJV)."*

Let's reread it in the Amplified Version:

"My people are destroyed for lack of knowledge: because you [the priestly nation] have rejected knowledge, I will also reject you that you shall be no priest to Me; seeing you have forgotten the law of your God, I will also forget your children (Hosea 4:6 AMP)."

If you read the Scripture above closely, you will notice there are consequences to spiritual ignorance.

I. "My people are destroyed because they lack knowledge!" Let's write it this way: "My people are ensnared, ravished by poverty and sickness because of their ignorance."

II. "...Because you [the priestly nation] have rejected knowledge, I will also reject you that you shall be no priest to me."

HOW TO UNLOCK THE BLESSING

The Bible emphatically declares that Jesus, *"And hast made us unto our God kings and priests: and we shall reign on the earth (Revelation 5:10)."*

This Scripture is true, but ignorance can displace you from your place of authority and stop you from reigning as king and priest as ordained by God. In the kingdom of God, we reign by knowledge, *"Jesus said, And ye shall know the truth, and the truth shall make you free (John 8:32)."*

Knowledge commands light. The absence of knowledge is the absence of light. When knowledge comes, light comes. Light is the master of darkness. Darkness does not compete with light. Once light appears, darkness disappears naturally. Lack of knowledge of the will of God is the reason a lot of believers are still laboring under the yoke of lack, poverty, and sickness. Paul understood this truth very well. That was the reason he prayed consistently for his converts to know (God's) will.

"That the God of our Lord Jesus Christ, the Father of glory, may give unto you the spirit of wisdom

and revelation in the knowledge of him: The eyes of your understanding being enlightened; that ye may know what is the hope of his calling, and what the riches of the glory of his inheritance in the saints, And what is the exceeding greatness of his power to us- ward who believe, according to the working of his mighty power (Ephesians 1:17 -19)."

"And this I pray, that your love may abound yet more and more in knowledge and in all judgment; That ye may approve things that are excellent; that ye may be sincere and without offence till the day of Christ (Philippians 1:9-10)."

2. PROSPERITY IS A CHOICE

God's will for you is prosperity. But if you do not believe in prosperity, it will not work in your life because God respects your authority regarding your choices.

"And I will give unto thee the keys of the kingdom of heaven: and whatsoever thou shalt bind on earth shall be bound in heaven: and whatsoever thou shalt loose on earth shall be loosed in heaven (Matthew 16:19)."

Everyone who carries THE BLESSING of the LORD ought to enjoy the blessings of God. Nonetheless, ignorance keeps many away from THE BLESSING and denies them access to the blessings of God. The blessings are on the pages of the Bible. Only those who search the word of God can discover them.

"This book of the law shall not depart out of thy mouth; but thou shalt meditate therein day and night, that thou mayest observe to do according to all that is written therein: for then thou shalt make thy way prosperous, and then thou shalt have good success (Joshua 1:8)."

You cannot 'recover' until you discover God's purpose for your life.

3. WRONG BELIEFS

One of the consequences of ignorance IS wrong belief. Ignorant people usually have false beliefs, often misinterpreting Scripture, misunderstanding God, and limited spiritual commitment. Erroneous belief retards THE BLESSING from manifesting in your life.

Paul spoke about the concept of 'wrong belief, he urged believers to *"Study to shew thyself approved unto God, a workman that needeth not to be ashamed, rightly dividing the word of truth (2 Timothy 2:15)."*

This example proves that because of ignorance, God's word is often mishandled. Usually, when the believer is ignorant of what a particular Scripture says. Paul expressed his concern over the wrong belief of the Galatians church in Galatians 1:6-7, *"I marvel that ye are so soon removed from him that called you into the grace of Christ unto another gospel: Which is not another; but there be some that trouble you, and would pervert the Gospel of Christ."*

The believers in Galatia knew the truth. They had accepted the Gospel of Grace, but soon after, some ignorant folks came to preach "another gospel," which contradicted what they had received. No doubt, this sudden change affected their attitude and character in the church. Consequently, they were no longer walking in love and faith, which are fundamental ingredients that reflect core Christian values. Having been entrapped by the spirit of "another gospel," the vulnerable brethren of the church in Galatia became critics of Paul and other brethren.

Wrong belief will deny you access to your covenant rights, hindering you from experiencing the power and manifestation of the Spirit in your life and ministry. False belief will deactivate your hope, neutralize your faith and replace it with fear. It will compromise your joy and clothe you in bitterness. Therefore, obedience is a major requirement in the manifestation of THE BLESSING of the LORD.

One of the ways to avoid becoming a victim is to study the Scripture yourself and stay away from people and teachings contrary to God's word. Instead, adopt the method of the Berean church.

"These were more noble than those in Thessalonica, in that they received the word with all readi-

ness of mind, and searched the scriptures daily, whether those things were so (Acts 17:11)."

Listening to and imbibing wrong teachings, keeping the wrong company, and visiting wrong places will corrupt you and endanger your faith. It will change you from being a man or woman of faith to an "unbelieving believer." The Bible says,

"He that walketh with wise men shall be wise: but a companion of fools shall be destroyed.... For as he thinketh In his heart, so is he..." (Proverbs 13:20; 23:7)

The danger associated with this kind of negative shift is that your faith, which is your spiritual currency, will malfunction, making you a liability instead of an asset and blessing to the kingdom of God and humanity.

4. DISOBEDIENCE

Disobedience is an act of failing or refusing to obey the instruction. Obedience is a primary requirement in our walk with God and the manifestation of THE BLESSING of the LORD. Obedience speaks of our love and commitment to God. Speaking in this regard, God said,

"But it shall come to pass, if thou wilt not hearken unto the voice of the LORD thy God, to observe to do all his commandments and his statutes which I command thee this day; that all these curses shall come upon thee, and overtake thee: (Deuteronomy 28: 15)."

"If ye be willing and obedient, ye shall eat the good of the land: But if ye refuse and rebel, ye shall be devoured with the sword: for the mouth of the LORD hath spoken it (Isaiah 1:19-20)."

Obedience was a significant requirement for the manifestation and continuous flow of THE BLESSING. That was the reason when Adam and Eve disobeyed God's instruction; THE BLESSING could not work maximally for them.

Also, when God called Abraham, He commanded him to leave the city of Ur and his family. But Abraham obeyed that instruction partially. He left the land of Ur, but he carried

THE BLESSINGS OF THE LORD

Lot along. This partial obedience hindered him greatly from experiencing the full manifestation of THE BLESSING of God.

"He did not experience full-blown prosperity until he obeyed God's instruction fully by separating from Lot. Now the LORD had said unto Abram, Get thee out of thy country, and from thy kindred, and from thy father's house, unto a land that I will shew thee: And I will make of thee a great nation, and I will bless thee, and make thy name great; and thou shalt be a blessing: And I will bless them that bless thee, and curse him that curseth thee: and in thee shall all families of the earth be blessed. So Abram departed, as the LORD had spoken unto him; and Lot went with him: and Abram was seventy and five years old when he departed out of Haran (Genesis 12:1-4)."

"And the LORD said unto Abram, after that Lot was separated from him, Lift up now thine eyes, and look from the place where thou art northward, and southward, and eastward, and westward: For all the land which thou seest, to thee will I give it, and to thy seed forever. And I will make thy seed as the dust of the earth: so that if a man can num-

ber the dust of the earth, then shall thy seed also be numbered. Arise, walk through the land in the length of it and in the breadth of it; for I will give it unto thee. Then Abram removed his tent, and came and dwelt in the plain of Mamre, which is in Hebron, and built there an altar unto the LORD (Genesis 13:14-18)."

The requirement of obedience to the Word of God is eternal. It is as essential in an era of grace as in the dispensations of innocence and the law. Adam and Eve lived before the dispensation of the law, yet God required obedience from them. Their inability to obey God led to their expulsion from the Garden of Eden. Disobedience is inconsistent with kingdom living. Every gift of God, including salvation, is free. But they must be received. Jesus came to this world and died on the cross to offer us salvation. We paid nothing to earn it. However, to experience the gift of salvation, we must receive it.

"For God so loved the world, that he gave his only begotten Son, that whosoever believeth in him should not perish, but have everlasting life (John 3:16)."

THE BLESSINGS OF THE LORD

"And this is the condemnation, that light is come into the world, and men loved darkness rather than light, because their deeds were evil (John 3:19)."

God does not force Himself and His gift on anyone because He respects our choices. Speaking in this regard, Jesus said, *"Behold, I stand at the door, and knock: if any man hear my voice, and open the door, I will come into him, and will sup with him, and he with me (Revelation. 3:20)."*

If you truly want to experience the manifestation of THE BLESSING of the LORD in your life, the following factors are very critical:

1. BELIEVE IT'S TRUE

Unbelief is an enemy of progress. You are not going to receive anything you are not sure is God's will for you. That is why you must search the Scripture to know the things freely given to us by God. THE BLESSING of the LORD is real. But you will never experience it except you believe it is real. The Psalmist said, *"I had fainted, unless I had believed to see the goodness of the LORD in the land of the living (Psalm 27:13)."*

2. HAVE FAITH IN GOD'S WORD

The Bible defines faith as *"...the substance of things hoped for, the evidence of things not seen (Hebrews 11:1)."* In other words, faith is to repose confidence in what we hope based on our fir, conviction, and assurance that the Lord is working behind the scene to bring it to pass, even though we cannot see it. Faith assures us that no matter the situation we are going through, the outcome shall be desirable. Against this backdrop, the Apostle Paul said, *"And we know that all things work together for good to them that love God, to them who are the called according to his purpose (Romans 8:28)."*

According to Kenneth Copeland, "Faith is the ability to believe without demanding proof. It is to believe because we have confidence or trust in the person who is speaking...." the five physical senses cannot define faith. Faith is a tangible force that affects the spiritual and natural world. The spirit of faith is believing and speaking as recorded in 2 Corinthians 4:13 NKJV thus, *"And since we have the same spirit of faith, according to what is written, 'I believed and therefore I spoke,' we also believe and therefore speak."*

God uses faith in all that He does. Faith in God is powerful and produces change." Nothing moves God like faith. Faith is putting your trust in God's ability to do what He had promised. Faith attracts God just the same way fear attracts the devil.

God does not ignore faith. When Jesus was physically present here on earth, he always responded to people who had faith for one miracle or the other. One practical example is the case of the woman with the issue of blood. The Bible says, *"And, behold, a woman, which was diseased with an issue of blood twelve years, came behind him, and touched the hem of his garment: For she said within herself, If I may but touch his garment, I shall be whole. But Jesus turned him about, and when he saw her, he said, Daughter, be of good comfort; thy faith hath made thee whole. And the woman was made whole from that hour (Matthew 9:20-22)."*

Oral Roberts defined faith thus, "When the Holy Spirit supernaturally empties you of doubt and fills you with a knowing, so at that moment you cannot doubt!" Your faith will be challenged several times, but keep your eyes on God. The easiest way to cultivate faith and strengthen it is to listen to the word of God. *"So then faith cometh by hearing, and hearing by the word of God (Romans 10:17)."* Fear comes by listening to the world. On the contrary, faith comes by hearing the word of God. Every man is a product of what he listens to often.

You will never experience Abraham's BLESSING until you put your faith to work. Nevertheless, Abraham received THE BLESSING by faith, so you cannot claim it otherwise.

"And he brought him forth abroad, and said, Look now toward heaven, and tell the stars, if thou be able to number them: and he said unto him, So shall thy seed be. And he believed in the LORD; and he counted it to him for righteousness (Genesis 15:5-6)."

The Blessings of the Lord

"For therein t s the righteousness of God revealed from faith to faith: as it is written, The just shall live by faith (Romans 1:17)."

Faith is the way to go. Faith is your anchor when you are drifting in the stormy sea of life.

3. MEDITATE ON THE WORD OF GOD

The word of God is the will of God for us. You cannot know what is accruable to your new status in Christ, except you discover it through a diligent search of the Scriptures. The word of God builds up and activates faith in our hearts. Through the word of God reveals our covenant BLESSING to us. Through faith, we actualize the promises of God in our lives. Therefore, develop the habit of studying and meditating on the word of God every day.

4. DECLARE THE BLESSING OVER YOUR LIFE

One of the most powerful truths in the Bible is that *"Words are spirit, and they are life (John 6:63)."* This powerful truth dropped from the mouth of Jesus Christ, the son of the living God. Therefore, nobody can dispute this fact. Words are not ordinary. They are bridges between the physical world and the spiritual world. Each time you speak, you either empower your angels or bind them: your words arc decrees or laws in the realm of the spirit. Therefore, be conscious of this fact. Your words will either bind you or set you free. Angels are ministering spirits sent to minister to the heirs of salvation. Every word you speak, they immediately go into action to bring it to pass for you. They see our words as an expression of our desires without minding whether they are good or bad. The Bible says, *"Are they not all ministering spirits, sent forth to minister for them who shall be heirs of salvation?" (Hebrews l:14)."*

The devil cannot defeat you without your permission because you are equipped and secured against his onslaught. However, negative confessions can create cracks in your wall of defense, allowing the devil to get to you. Job was heavily and powerfully equipped and defended by God. But, unfortunately, he allowed fear and negative confessions to rob him of God's protection and divine covering. The Bible says, *"And it was so, when the days of their feasting were gone about, that Job sent and sanctified them, and rose up early in the morning, and offered burnt offerings according to the number of them all: for Job said, It may be that my sons have sinned, and cursed God in their hearts. Thus did Job continually (Job 1:5)."*

How did the devil know that Job was afraid? He knew it through his negative confessions. *"For Job said, it may be that my sons have sinned, and cursed God in their hearts...thus did Job continually."* Later, he said, *"For the thing which I greatly feared is come upon me, and that which I was afraid of is come unto me. I was not in safety, neither had I rest, neither was I quiet; yet trouble came (Job 3:25-26)."*

Have you seen that? Fear and negative confessions became a pattern in his life until they brought him calamities. In one of her books, Gloria Copeland said,

"Once you have prayed, acted on God's word, and believed that you had received the answers, demand that your actions, thoughts, and words agree with what you have received. Act as though you have it. Satan knows that unless he can get you to change your confession of faith, his hold over you is broken. If Satan had any authority of his own, he would not have to depend on deception. Satan has to trick you into saying what he wants to come to pass. Did you know that Satan can only do what you say? Let me repeat that: All that Satan can do is what you say."

Put a watch on your mouth and determine not to speak in agreement with the devil and your circumstances. The Spirit of the Lord and THE BLESSING of the LORD respond to faith, not fear.

5. PRAYER

Prayer is more than talking to God. It is an opportunity to have fellowship with God. It is the time to have communion with God. Prayer is putting God in remembrance of His Word. THE BLESSING is a product of the Spirit, whereas prayer is the key to the spirit world. In other words, prayer is the key that unlocks the supernaturaL

The Blessings of the Lord

You cannot unleash THE BLESSING without generating sufficient power through prayers. Abraham was a man of the Spirit. He built many altars where he fellowshipped with God. The Bible says,

"And the LORD appeared unto Abram, and said, Unto thy seed will I give this land: and there built he an altar unto the LORD, who appeared unto him. And he removed from thence unto a mountain on the east of Bethel, and pitched his tent, having Bethel on the west, and Hai on the east: and there he built an altar unto the LORD, and called upon the name of the LORD (Genesis 12:7-8)."

Nothing works in the kingdom without prayer. Jesus stated that prayer ought to be our attitude or lifestyle. *"And he spake a parable unto them to this end, that men ought always to pray, and not to faint (Luke 18:1)."*

The quality of your prayer (fellowship with God) determines the value God places on it and the result you will get. For example, two identical twins may kneel at the altar to pray. While one prays for her personal needs, the other focuses on interceding for the harvest of souls into the kingdom, anointing for the pastor of her local church, national revival, world leaders.

As you can see, although the two sisters above prayed passionately together at the altar for an hour, their burden and focus were quite different. Between the both of them, who do you think God will reward most? The honest answer is that God will reward the second sister more because she has a global mindset and understands the heartbeat of God concerning soul-winning and harvest of souls into His kingdom.

"Then saith he unto his disciples, The harvest truly is plenteous, but the labourers are few; Pray ye therefore the Lord of the harvest, that he will send forth labourers into his harvest (Matthew 9:37-38)."

While praying for one's need is highly commendable, we should move forward and develop a personal burden expressed through prayers to ensure the fulfillment of God's desire. In Mark

16:15-16, *"And he said unto them, Go ye into all the world, and preach the Gospel to every creature. He that believeth and is baptized shall be saved; but he that believeth not shall be damned."*

"And how shall they preach, except they be sent? as it is written, How beautiful are the feet of them that preach the Gospel of peace, and bring glad tidings of good thingsn(Romans 10:15)!"

GOD HAS A NEED; ARE YOU AWARE?

Not many believers know that God has a need! God in His wisdom has structured the earth so that the creation depends on Him for their provisions. This structure invariably makes prayer a critical factor in the school of success and our relationship with God. Jesus admonished the disciples to pray always (Luke 18:1). Someone may ask: *"If something is the will of God, do we still need to pray about it? The answer is in the affirmative. Jesus categorically taught His disciples in Matthew 6 to pray for God's will to be done on earth. "After this manner therefore pray ye: Our Father which art in heaven, Hallowed be thy name.*

Thy kingdom come. Thy will be done in earth, as it is in heaven (Matthew 6:9-10)."

In Luke 2:25-32, 36-38, you will observe that although Simeon and Anna, the prophetess knew that the coming of the Messiah to this world was the will of God yet they engaged the altar of prayer vigorously until the Messiah was born. If you want to experience the fullness of THE BLESSING of the LORD, spend quality time with the Lord in prayers. Prayer is worship! Prayer shows that you have acknowledged Him as your Lord and only source.

6. TITHE AND SEED YOUR FAITH

Tithe is the beginning of financial wisdom. It is the gateway to financial freedom. It is one of the ways of activating the covenant of economic prosperity. The Bible asked a pertinent question thus: *"Will a man rob God? Yet ye have robbed me. But ye say, werein have we robbed thee? In tithes and offerings. Ye are cursed with a curse: for ye have robbed me, even this whole nation (Mal. 3:8-9)."*

THE BLESSINGS OF THE LORD

I would like you to read what the great evangelist, author, and teacher of our time, Oral Roberts, said concerning tithe and seed-faith:

"The basic beginning of financial wisdom IS when we get into the spirit of giving with joy and expectation. But, suppose my ministry and yours do not continually plant the seeds of tithes, offering and helping the unfortunate. In that case, we will never reap the miracle harvest that the Lord intended for our lives and our ministries. Never!"

A rejected (or neglected) opportunity to pay tithe or sow seeds of faith is a lost opportunity to receive a miracle harvest, including financial harvests. We see from Abram's example in Genesis 14:18-20 that giving tithe is not an option. It is the earthly manifestation of the seed of our faith. God says, *"The just shall live by faith (Romans 1:17)."*

God's spiritual laws of sowing and reaping are all predicated on our faith. As for me, once I saw this, I realized we gain THE BLESSING of Abraham by tithing, and we grow by giving.

From Hebrews 7, we know that Melchizedek is a type of Jesus. I have been faithful to give tithes of all my finances as my seed faith. Receiving THE BLESSING - not just a blessing - has made all the difference in my life and ministry. Knowledge commands light. The absence of knowledge is the absence of light

It is true that you can gain without following the Bible's principles of giving and receiving or sowing and reaping. But in the final analysis, your wallet will still have holes in it.

Divine principles can work anywhere. It worked for Abraham, Oral Robert, me (Apostle Bala), and thousands of other covenant- practitioners. If you practice the same principles, you will have the same result and amazing testimonies.

In chapter 6, we shall see THE BLESSING working wonders in the lives of those who believe in this covenant.

CHAPTER 6

IT WORKS

"Christ hath redeemed us from the curse of the law, being made a curse for us: for it is written, Cursed is everyone that hangeth on a tree: That the blessing of Abraham might come on the Gentiles through Jesus Christ; that we might receive the promise of the Spirit through faith." — Galatians 3:13-14

Many people still doubt the potency of THE BLESSING of the LORD to deliver in our generation. The real problem such people have is a lack of knowledge.

"My people are destroyed for lack of knowledge: because thou hast rejected knowledge, I will also reject thee, that thou shalt be no priest to me: see-

ing thou hast forgotten the law of thy God, I will also forget thy children (Hosea 4:6)."

They are ignorant of the simple fact that Abraham's covenant is everlasting. They fail to understand that through Christ, we have been engrafted into the family of Abraham, thereby becoming an heir of Abraham's BLESSING.

The blessing is as potent today as when God first pronounced it upon Adam, Noah, and Abraham. Moreover, God has made it more real today through His son, Jesus Christ, than any other time in the history of humanity. The testimonies below further confirm the potency and effectiveness of THE BLESSING of the LORD in our days.

I must confess that I did not see many miracles in my ministry before I discovered the covenant of THE BLESSING of the LORD. I labored under the yoke of ignorance like many pastors do for a long time. God in His mercy gave me little result here and there. But when the Holy Spirit taught me about THE BLESSING and empowered me with it, things began to happen supernaturally in my ministry. Since then, deliverance, healing, signs, and wonders have become regular occurrences in my life and ministry.

For example, we have seen the dead raised back to life, the yoke of abject poverty in people's lives broken, and their lives transformed. We have seen people with hopeless situations restored and established. We have seen our church members delivered from boarding an aircraft that later crashed-landed through divine intervention, killing all the passengers. Through the empowerment of THE BLESSING, we have seen God's backing in our missionary journey. We have witnessed prostitutes surrender to Christ, getting married, and preaching the Gospel. We have seen people of the worst character give their lives to Christ and preach the Gospel. Let's look at a few of these testimonies. They were all made possible by the Spirit of God after my encounter with the BLESSING of the LORD.

RAISED FROM DEAD

When I was on missionary work to the city of Port Harcourt in the southern part of Nigeria, one day, my landlord's son (Danison) died. Expectedly, there was pandemonium everywhere. People were wailing and lamenting with such agony that shook heaven. Like all other tenants and neighbors, I wondered what could have brought about such a sudden death. But when I couldn't stand the tears of the boy's parents and neighbors as they were flowing down their cheeks freely, I was moved by the Spirit of God and deep compassion in my heart to pray for the boy. So I took my prayer team and entered the room where Danison's body lay.

As we entered the room, the power of THE BLESSING began to work. After a time of interceding and calling on the spirit of the young man to return, the Holy Spirit jerked him back to life, and we handed him alive to his parents.

STRANGE DISEASE DISAPPEARED

A wealthy woman came to me for prayer. She had a disease that had destroyed her immune system for 20 years, to be precise. In her desperation, she visited both orthodox and traditional medicine practitioners, including churches and prayer houses, and they all did their best, but all to no avail. She even had several surgeries, but all those efforts proved abortive. Finally, however, when she came to me for prayer, the Spirit of God helped me to know that her problem was spiritual. So, after praying and anointing her with oil, God healed her. That was the last time she experienced the attack.

DELIVERANCE FROM PLANE CRASH

In 1996, God told me to call for a 7-day vigil with Holy Communion to stop members of my congregation from untimely death through a plane crash. I did not understand the depth of the revelation at that time. But I decided to carry out the instruction. I informed the congregation about the impending danger and what God instructed us to do. Ten of my members bought the ticket of that company to fly with that ill-fated plane. But amazingly, they missed their flight. One of them was so angry that he planned to sack his driver for delaying failing to pick him up from the airport for a crucial meeting. But that plane crashed midway to its destination, killing everyone on board. It was indeed difficult times in our nation's history for these plane crash victims and their families. THE BLESSING of the LORD is not limited to material blessing. It is a power that enables you to have dominion in the air, land, and sea. It is comprehensive life insurance for the total man.

THE BLIND RECEIVED HER SIGHT

My chief usher quarreled with one of her neighbors. Her neighbor decided to attack her through diabolical power instead of peaceful dialogue to settle the matter. This lady (my chief usher) became sick suddenly and eventually became blind. When I heard about this pathetic situation, I was provoked in the spirit and went to pray for her. I followed the instructions God gave me while praying for her, and her sight was restored. However, the blindness returned to her neighbor, who attacked her with the blindness, and she became blind immediately. THE BLESSING of the LORD gives you dominion over powers of darkness.

THE BLESSINGS OF THE LORD

HARLOTS TURNED EVANGELISTS

A lady who was a prostitute attended one of our services. In the course of the service, I led her to the Lord. She did not only receive Christ as her Lord and Saviour but the Holy Spirit. After her salvation experience, she refused to go back to the hotel where she lived with her colleagues. The church supported her financially to take care of herself. She later took us to where her former colleagues were living, and we preached Christ to them. Almost a hundred of these young girls surrendered their lives to Christ.

After I taught them about THE BLESSING of the LORD and how to work in dominion, they received the revelation, and they all got married. Some of them are married to Europeans. The good news is that they carried the fire of the revival to everywhere they went. One of them never fails to send me a gift (every year) on my birthday, 14th February. THE BLESSING can work in the life of everyone who is born again and willing to walk in obedience.

IT WORKS

A TOMATO MERCHANT

After I finished preaching in one of our services, I prophesied over a particular woman in the service. I called her out and told her to resign from her job and start selling tomatoes. Whenever I share this testimony, I always caution pastors not to attempt this except the Spirit of God leads them. After much inner struggle borne out of fear, the woman decided to obey the voice of the Spirit. It didn't take long when God turned around her situation. She built a 2-story building. To date, THE BLESSING of the LORD is working in her life.

FROM SELLING BREAD TO CRUDE OIL

Another of our pastors came to our church for healing because of the deadly sickness on her body. When I saw her, I was moved by the Spirit to pray for her. Like the previous testimony, I told her to stop selling bread and look for another business as directed by the Holy Spirit. I gave her a token of five hundred Naira after praying over it as a point of contact for her new business. She left with a heart full of faith. Not too long after that, God miraculously connected her to someone who helped her start a crude oil business. Today, she is one of the wealthiest people in her community.

SUPERNATURAL LIFTING

One of our younger church members sowed a seed after listening to me preach on "FAITH IN THE WORD OF GOD." So I prayed for him and prophesied that in due time, God would make him a millionaire. To the glory of God, it did not take long when this prophecy came to pass in his life.

On my Birthday Thanksgiving Service, which our Lagos church organized on my behalf, this young boy donated five hundred thousand Naira effortlessly towards the ceremony.

Friend, THE BLESSING of the LORD is real. If it works for others, it will also work for you. Therefore, get ready to manifest your sonship.

CHAPTER 7

Apostolic and Prophetic Declarations

"Again he said unto me, Prophesy upon these bones, and say unto them, O ye dry bones, hear the word of the LORD. Thus saith the Lord GOD unto these bones; Behold, I will cause breath to enter into you, and ye shall live." — Ezekiel 37:4-5

Abraham never knew God had made him the possessor of heaven and earth through THE BLESSING He put upon him. It was the declaration made by Melchizedek that awoken him to that reality.

THE BLESSINGS OF THE LORD

Destinies were designed by God but unleashed by men in the hope of ensuring their fulfillment. In His mercy and wisdom, God has raised apostles, prophets, evangelists, pastors, and teachers to equip His children until they grow into spiritual maturity and fulfill their call in life and ministry. If these ministry gifts were not necessary, God would not raise them.

Apostles and prophets have special assignments in the program of God, especially in fulfilling the great commission and setting free those who are bound and granting them direction in life by the leading of the Holy Spirit. The Bible says, *"And by a prophet the LORD brought Israel out of Egypt, and by a prophet was he preserved (Hosea 12:13)."*

As stated earlier, Melchizedek's declaration over Abraham opened his eyes of understanding regarding his new status and positioned him on a spiritual pedestal of faith that qualified him to receive the fullness of God's promises concerning him.

Apostolic and Prophetic Declarations

Many Christians are like the dry bones in Ezekiel 37. They can't become the mighty army that God created them to become. They need someone who has a higher apostolic or prophetic unction to unlock THE BLESSING and call out their destinies into existence. That was what Ezekiel did to those dry bones in the valley. Similarly, that was what Moses did for the tribe of Reuben after he came under the curse of his father, Jacob.

"Reuben, thou art my firstborn, my might, and the beginning of my strength, the excellency of dignity, and the excellency of power: Unstable as water, thou shalt not excel; because thou wentest up to thy father's bed; then defiledst thou it: he went up to my couch (Genesis 49:3-4)."

"Let Reuben live, and not die; and let not his men be few (Deuteronomy 33:6 KJV)."

Elijah did the same thing for Elisha (2 Kings 9-14). Paul did the same thing for young Timothy (1 Timothy 4:14). Declarations and affirmations empowered all these people. But, unless someone with a higher anointing calls into exis-

The Blessings of the Lord

tence THE BLESSING of the LORD in your life, you may not realize your full potential till you leave this earth.

Before I end this book, I want to speak over your life and call your glorious destiny into existence to begin to work for you. I want the glory of God to be seen all over you and your household.

To this end, I yield myself unto God as His chosen instrument, the apostle of Jesus Christ and a prophet to nations. Thus, I unlock THE BLESSING of the LORD in your life and call your glory into existence.

1. Your glorious dream shall come to pass; you shall fulfill your destiny.

2. I unlock THE BLESSING OF THE LORD in your life and call your glory into existence.

3. I command the dry bones in your life to come back together and become a mighty army. Henceforth, your life will have a positive shape.

Apostolic and Prophetic Declarations

4. I speak to your skills, talents, and business. Let them begin to attract help and helpers to join you in Jesus' Name.

5. I call your helpers across the globe to locate and help you in Jesus' Name.

6. Nothing will cut your life short. I decree there will be no loss of life, property, finances, divine connection.

7. I speak to the triangular powers of the sun, moon, and stars to intercept and destroy every evil arrow fired at you, your loved ones, and finances in Jesus' Name.

8. I release you and all that God has given to you from every satanic prison and cauldron.

9. If you are seeking God for your life partner, I place a demand on the angel of the Lord, and I call upon the Spirit of God to bring you and your spouse together and bless you with godly children.

The Blessings of the Lord

10. I speak to the earth to yield her fatness to you, "The profit of the earth is for all: the king himself is served by the field." (Ecclesiastes 5:9) Therefore, I speak to the earth to profit you in the Name of Jesus.

11. I declare that the Lord shall make you fruitful in every good thing you do. You shall loan to nations, and you shall not borrow.

12. I summon all the powers that have held you captive and deprived you of enjoying the benefits of your new birth in Christ. I judge them by the power in the blood of Jesus, *"And they overcame him by the blood of the lamb, and by the word of their testimony...(Revelation 12:11)."*

13. Today, I release the fire of judgment upon any spiritual image that walks with you or has sex with you in the dream, thereby draining you of spiritual strength. By the power in the blood of Jesus, I separate them from you forever.

14. I curse every sickness and disease in your body and cast them out in the Name of Jesus.

Apostolic and Prophetic Declarations

15. Every evil mark on your body is erased by the blood of Jesus.

16. I declare that every case or transaction you may have with the government, any organization, or individual will end in your favor.

17. Any man or woman who closes in on you to defraud or harm you shall be exposed and arrested by the Holy Ghost in the Name of Jesus.

18. Every project you have started according to God's divine plan for your life shall be concluded with speed by the finger of God.

19. I declare that both heaven and earth will unite together to bring these prophetic declarations to pass in your life shortly in Jesus' mighty name.

Go and be fruitful and multiply, fill the earth and subdue it, have dominion, and reign as king and priest in the affairs of life.

Congratulations!
Congratulations!!

THE BLESSINGS OF THE LORD

Congratulations!!!

Keep soaring, keep rejoicing, keep celebrating and keep loving God.

I Love You!

About The Author

Dr. Bala Success Abraham (BSA) is the Found or Apostolic Triumphant Church Internation, located in several parts of the world, including the United States of America, South Africa, and Nigeria. He is also the Founder and Internation President of the Apostolic Team Internation (ATI) – the arm of the ministry responsible for reaching out to clergy in Africa and other parts of the world.

Dr. Abraham loves the Lord! He is a man of the Holy Spirit, an Apostle, Prophet, and reacher of the Word of God.

Dr. Bala Abraham is the President and Chief Executive Officer of Bala Success Global. This Foundation sponsors children for school, provide medical assistance, food, shelter, and clothing for those in need.

OTHER BOOKS BY APOSTLE DR. BALA SUCCESSABRAHAM

"Power To Raise Destiny From The Grave"
"Signs And Wonders Of The Holy Spirit"
"Revealed Knowledge Of God In The Blood Of Jesus"
"Rivers Of Gladness"

If this book has blessed you, text or write me. I want to share in your joy and testimonies.

www.ingramcontent.com/pod-product-compliance
Lightning Source LLC
Chambersburg PA
CBHW071503070526
44578CB00001B/429